POINT OF NO RETURN

Anne Valley-Fox

Point
of
No
Return

P O E M S

For Gary —
In poetry + friendship.

LA ALAMEDA PRESS :: ALBUQUERQUE

Anne Valley-Fox

These poems first appeared in the following publications:
"Viaje al Sur" and "Any Tear in the Social Fabric" in *Sin Fronteras/Writers without Borders*; "A Conversation," "After Seven Years," "Down in the Arms of the Blues," "In Love You Must Come Where He Is," "It Falls to Me," "Lonesome Song," "Love in a Dream the Color of Blood," "Sex & the Lake," "10,000 Joys 10,000 Sorrows," "Wine Song" and "It Falls to Me" in *Fish Drum Magazine*; "After Seven Years" in *In Company: An Anthology of New Mexico Poets after 1960* (University of New Mexico); "& Now We Are Moving Our Household" in the e-zine *LA Poetry Festival*; "Some Days," "What He Left Me," and "What Is Given" in *Manzanita Quarterly*; "Pneumonia," "Cyclops," "Cats," "My Husband, Just Returned from a Visit to Havana," "Extramarital Sex," "Point of No Return," "Changing of the Guard," "(But You Could Never Afford It)," "Penelope Dreams the Seashore," "When You Meet Your Former Husband on the Road," "Woman Y," and "Ordinary News" in the e-zine *Santa Fe Poetry Broadside*; "My Husband, Just Returned from a Visit to Havana" in *THE*.

Cover art: "The Suicide" by Bruce Lowney
color lithograph, 16 x 23 inches, copyright © 1984

Book design by J. Bryan

ISBN: 1-888809-46-9

Library of Congress Cataloging-in-Publication Data:
Valley-Fox, Anne.
 Point of no return : poems / Anne Valley-Fox.
 p. cm.
 ISBN 1-888809-46-9 (alk. paper)
 I. Title.

PS3556.O876P65 2004
811'.54--dc22

                           2004021069

La Alameda Press
9636 Guadalupe Trail NW
Albuquerque, NM 87114

Contents

I often want to say to people, "You have neat, tight expectations of what life ought to give you, but you won't get it." That isn't what life does. Life does not accommodate you, it shatters you. It is meant to, and it couldn't do it better. Every seed destroys its container or else there would be no fruition.

—*Florida Scott-Maxwell*
THE MEASURE OF MY DAYS

Viaje al Sur

You wake each day to a different place—
thrum of traffic or surf breaking?

Light tightens the white-washed walls
of elephant palms, campfire ash, spoons
stabbed into sand.

A pair of macaws alights on a post, squawking in Spanish.
It is as if you married in passion one afternoon
and wake beside a stranger.

Your husband rises, stumbles about, connecting the dots
between objects and vegetation.

A village daughter of six or seven
steps into camp, intrepid and shy, hawking
her mama's tamales.

Your child shakes out his woven shoes,
checking for scorpions.

My Husband, Just Returned from a Visit to Havana

Gifts of coffee and fine cigars, Cuban rum
mellow as cognac, all stripped of conspicuous labels
mound the table between us.

Odalisque island reclines on a hip
her sinuous spine, east to west, rippling
mountains and rivers.

My courier's eyes are the shirred gray
of blown cloud. I borrow from them—
musical streets
Communist rubble
prostitutes in mango dresses
voluble children and men
on the make—their skin the luscious flavors of
figs and dates.

Cuba calls my husband back.
His admiration shows me a cobra extending itself
for the charmer.
He loved her at once because
she is not his country.
I try to remember: When did I depart
the isle of romance?
And pater-dictator, Fidel at a distance—how frivolous
now to be faithful!

Oh Cuba, beautiful girl, stop your singing,
this man comes running—believe me, I know him,
he's yours.

Perfume

(i)
Nile barge sails drenched in gardenias
the path to the Queen's bed rivers the lover's ankles
in rose petals. Her royal pulses murmur
sandalwood, frankincense, lavender, myrrh—
a map of the Orient.

(ii)
You come to bed smelling of Chinese take-out
and wood shavings. I've covered my bases with baby powder,
a dozen years on the shelf. Wooly endearments
slip from our lips—your left arm, warm from the heart,
stalls across my ribs.

(iii)
I think the air remembers . . . Cleopatra's
cinnamon breath, moisture of viper curled in papyrus—as we
are inhaling Rose of Damascus, petals plucked by the Queen's
servants, their hands dark with neroli oil,
plumping her lover's pillow.

You Call Me Your Flower

You call me your flower: daisy, dahlia,
wild rose, petaled lips

blown to the neck, scent of cedar
and cracked leather

juiced on composting earth.
Deciduous joy

sluices the bellows: Vision may dim,
then sharpen its edges again.

In Love You Must Come Where He Is

In love you must come where he is: pull up
a chair, rest your arms on the blade splintered table
and wait—never mind crazed birds hurling themselves
against the house, committees phoning, thuds in the attic,
the kids begging money to go to the movies—

Don't move. Steady your nerves with a cup of coffee.
Pour one for him, speak in glyphs, watch his hands
pinch tobacco, drizzle a paper square. Apricot branches
scraping the window telegraph human atrocities
on every continent. You must not

embrace them, nor tender the ghosts of carnal incineration.
Time swirls in numinous slivers around the body.
Come where he is, piping love through the flutes of
your bones—at last he reaches across the table
offering bread, buttered for you to eat.

A Conversation

"The descent beckons / as the ascent beckoned."
—William Carlos Williams

Impatient, she prods him: "But anyone's life
is a staircase or arc—perilous waste
stretching away—we're all going
down in the dark!"

Years before she would have coaxed: "Darling,
come closer!" stroking along the natural grain, but now
she's contracted: "Don't you realize it's hell
or high water?"

At length he replies: "Even before a trap springs
the breath catches, floorboards buckle, you stumble
and a gaff from the underworld
snatches at your ankles."

& Now We Are Moving Our Household

My life is a blind of mismatched chairs
& unlabeled boxes delivered to
random rooms—*O Muse,*
promise you'll never leave me!

I know I'm the least of your pupils, my
aspirations are stained with phenomena—stuff
that will end up in homeless shelters,
mostly.

I'm badly distracted by vanity &
the wreckage of social justice. I bite my nails,
color my hair, kid myself with tequila.
My children are experts at walking through

walls; I pummel them with cliché.
Mine will be an obituary
smoky with loaves of bread burning.
Nevertheless

you welcome me
home—I loll in a jumble of dawn-pinked
pillows, winnowing syllables, ersatz grain, above
your windy fields.

Cats

You argue bitterly, resolution
Impossible—

The cat springs from the back of the stove
As you turn on the burner.

She curls beneath the easy chair.
She will have none of this foolishness.

The accusation flings itself:
"You don't understand me!"

He knows, in fact, how to please you, but
Refuses. And vice versa.

The cat licks her bristled fur—
And you ask another to do this for you!

Down in the Arms of the Blues

for S.W.

Across a table shimmering girl, black hat,
golden hair, hands like doves: "Perhaps
there are only imagined impediments. Broken-
legged, you walk on your hands, invent a vita,
ask for what you need—on earth, this works."
Older woman feels whittled down, in her
plentiful flesh, to a stick. The path winds dimly
ahead and behind. Her husband is frail &
unemployed; he fumes over broken instruments
& houseplants sprouting in water to no
effect. She sets down her soupspoon & lights
a cigarette, phosphorous sweet on the matchstick.
She watches the girl pluck up the check with
lavender painted nails. Biting on smoke,
she taps off a tower of ash.

Lonesome Song

Kind to each other—
yet rarely now
do we leap

chasms, meet
mid-air between
our drifting

moons.
It's
problem enough

to inhabit one's
private planet.
But oh, it gets

lonesome—
doesn't it,
dear?

Cyclops

She stands at the stove in a 50s wrap,
a gaggle of little girls.

Human monster moves in tight, eyes overlapped,
vise-gripping her waist.

"You don't look the same!" he accuses.

The biggest girl comes swinging at him
from behind. The woman plunges a long handled spoon
down the rage of his throat—
for good measure, her thumbs and forefingers
stab at his eyes, fishing for
slippery plums.

He gags, topples backwards.

Why did the monster offer so little resistance?
What about her has changed?

Love in a Dream the Color of Blood

A woman becomes betrothed
to a killer. A slight
charismatic man, he
lifts his metallic
phallus with casual
grace, sites the hostage
dragged before him &
squeezes: collapsing
backwards, the
victim's shirtfront
reddens with roses.
This woman has
made of her man
a lover—tender,
solicitous, innocent of
her brooding intent
to leave him.
At times she feels heavy, inert
as an anchor, unworthy of
action—or else
she's cyclonic, quick to
cleanse & destroy.
She shams like
a child, eyes
squeezed, toy gun cocked
at the hottest star.

She Warned Him to Keep His Hands

She warned him to keep his hands
out of the hair of the woman
standing in front of him
on the bleachers, locks cascading
in chestnut chains to the waist.
Shamed or in sharp avoidance, he
conceded—

Yet soon as his jailer turned away
he plunged his hands in that
protein wealth to the
wrists, elbows, neck—he
spooled, stroked, jack-knifed, jetted,
gasping for breath, Macbeth in his sudsy
ardor, mad to come clean.

Truce

(i)
Smoke rolling over the mountain
nothing happens for several years
after the violent eruption

(ii)
Snatching little sips of air
all the villagers nervously glad
she is cooling her heels

Extramarital Sex

A masochist trained in extravagant feats of mind over matter
sat in a box for 24 hours in deep meditation
while thousands of scorpions made themselves at home
on his person: backs of his knees, between his toes, his groin, neck,
eyelashes, scalp, etcetera.

You were recalling the scorpion king
before you fell asleep last night and so in your dream
you took a spider into your mouth and right away
she bit you. Your tongue ballooned so you could barely phone me:
"A black widow bit my tongue—help me!"
But I refused. "You put the venomous thing in your mouth—
you take the consequences."

I feel ashamed, when you tell me the dream, not to have
come to your aid. I might have saved you. I might have redeemed
our relations. But fucking A, how dumb can you get—
taking a thing you know to be deadly
into your mouth like that?

Point of No Return

What was the critical border
crossed, corner
turned,
bridge burned behind us?

Collapse may follow
crisis, like
the fall of Rome:

                    grain shortages
                                        slave revolt
                                                        invasions
                assassinations—

The emperor, forgetting himself
becomes a combatant,
stages a bloodbath, burns
the city down.

Where is the point of no return?
No one sees it coming or
can tell you when.

There Comes a Crack in the Mudded Hut of Consciousness

There comes a crack in the mudded hut of consciousness
when one who spun your dross into gold
shows you the man
he's become: cold feet; ambivalence with a chip on its
shoulder; runaway crushes on lone women in produce aisles
fondling apples and eggplants.

There comes a crack so piercingly slender, you may not notice:
your arms, that bundled this marriage together, ache
to release. You dwell instead on obstructions:
children, illness, debt, in-laws, marital vows (those rotated
fields stretching across Kansas), your
stubborn refusal to lose.

The moment he clears his throat: "There's something
I need to tell you—"
shock yourself twice! Agree
to dissolve on a razor's edge, turn sideways
and squeeze through the fissure—quickly, before the wound
closes over.

Outside mudded cloister walls, you read by touch
the language of fissure, seeking
hermetic secrets.
What made you blind? Why did you woo oblivion?
What is the piece that slipped through your fingers, the crack
in your hovel of love?

Marriage Boat (A Study in Perspective)

(i)
Sea-slashed, becalmed,
disturbed at times from the deeps, you
work the ropes in tandem
to stay afloat.

(ii)
Dry-dock the boat, part
company, razor out his coordinates and
your errors are glaring; his,
unforgivable.

The Camel Driver

The camel driver saddles his beast
with oddities, objects

he hopes to convert to gold
in a foreign land.

He seems to be leaving behind
the essentials—don't ask their names—

he hid them in the deep caves of his loins.
I'm glad he is going, this camel driver.

I didn't want him
camped in my field, sorting his wares,

smoking me dry with his cooking fires.

Our Old House

Our old house has the look of a sickbed moiled
by fever, or maybe a homestead
abandoned by vandals—mud tracks, choked
toilets, smashed plastic appliances.

The new owners have already come, a breezy
couple and triplet of little girls. "The early bird
catches the worm!" the woman exudes.
Furiously, I hurry from room to room.

When you arrive with a pack of boys, you
chide me for barking work orders
at clumps of slack-jawed adolescents
lounging on blowzy sofas. "Go

fuck yourself," I hiss.
My hands are rushing to clear a surface of disparate
objects: some I push into dresser drawers,
others fall to my pockets.

Though fucking yourself is something you might enjoy.
My Scottish ancestors back me up, lining the hall
in black and white: starched collars, punishing lips,
our dark, unyielding hearts.

Penelope Dreams a Reunion

He shows me into his library
built to seduce: mahogany shelves, books
to the eaves, laddered balconies, lilies.
I'm rocked by remorse.
Could closer attention be given?
Look what you've thrown to the dogs!

We wander into the sun room.
I open my blouse, he pulls off his clothes
we fall on the chaise in buttery light
locked together, unmoving.
Abruptly he's up and roaming the room
speaking a lost language.
Shipwrecked, I lie in the gutted space
of his naked grace.

He doesn't know he has gone from this place—
he will never get back.

(But You Could Never Afford It)

I thought I wanted to be your wife & did
my damndest (bamboo roots

stubborn as sin
underpinning the garden) but

obsession's a sorry substitute
for knack.

Overripe to play the mistress, I could be
your whore!

You'd like that, I'll bet—100 bucks
on your way out the door

& you'd never have to
fix anything.

Changing of the Guard

San Felipe Pueblo: *Casino Hollywood*
equidistant from A to Z
a couple of semis idle their engines
down in the bottom lot
a few minutes late
we beat him by 10
ex-husband noses his truck
beside my car
cranks the window:
"Sorry I'm late . . . how're you doing?"

Teenager already out of the car
backpack tossed
in the bed of the truck
runs interference: "Mom went totally nuts
this morning, she threw
a spoon at me!"
For what it's worth, I set the record
straight: "I threw it *near* you, not
at you, my dear—and it was a fork,
not a spoon."

You Force Me to Speak in Clichés

It's you, again,
papering roses the size of your fists
to the flanks of anonymous rooms,
a contract which bores you
silly—

I think of the butcher stuffing apples
into a pig's mouth.

You say you'd like to go spelunking
with me and the others.
How to explain the rules of the new terrain?
The reach is wrong for yelling
or reading lips. Listen:

Life is not a bowl of cherries;
your roses, old love, have thorns.

Over the Mountain

(i)
Motorcycles shaving the road
my oldest son
and your brother-in-law

drop back—you take the lead—
aspen clap
mountain curves peeled
like perfect apples.

Halfway up
around a bend
the others brake—skid
to a stop:

metal engulfed
by pyre of flames
billowing over the tarmac.

But thrown to the shoulder—
miraculous!
you're on your feet
staring, stupefied
into the conflagration.

(ii)
I am roasting chiles for supper
when you return.
"How was the ride?"
Your fellow travelers avert their eyes.
"Thrilling," you deadpan.

A week elapses before I notice
the absence.
"Where is your bike?"
You toss me the nut in its shell:
"Up in flames."

(iii)
You were my chosen beloved!
You might have contained me
made me wiser
pried me open to each
burning occasion.

Instead you are donning a white
tuxedo, wedding
another.

(iv)

I don't forgive you
your intimate betrayals.

One day I mean to,
though.

We'll meet in the street
and I will be burning
the cold fire of angels.

I'll bandy your latter-day name.
"The business between us
is finished—"

and you will disperse
like smoke over the mountain.

What He Left Me

He left me a Burmese Buddha
A mala of wooden beads
Green tile flaking grout
Pain in the ass piling up paperwork
One old car (burns oil)
One beautiful son
Profound disturbance
His way of writing the number 8 like stacking a snowman
Ex-inlaws sending me cheese
Family photos spilled from shelves
A kitchen idea: use a separate chopping block for garlic and onions
A realization: hot love burns fast—

He left me a pizza stone
A colander
Philosophy books nibbled by mice in the shed
A dog who cries
A string of pearls
A digging shovel
A gimp wheelbarrow
Artesian well of dream image
An empty bed
The gaze of men
A skiff I have christened *Sexual Union*
A habit to break: Quit reading his damn horoscope—

He left me silence (like peace of mind)—and a son, a son, a son!

After Seven Years

(i)
After seven years the dyes have surrendered
to light—marigold bleached yellow, sapphire
clouded, ruby the yawning pink of blood
dripped into buckets of water.
Snags in the weave give us
something to work—nubbed thorns in the olive
grove, the unraveled tip of an arrow, wing cartilage
ripped below the scapula.

(ii)
Doe, slowing, brittle with anguish
turns at the edge of the wood. "You might have
caught me but you were distracted by
nymphs & the weight of your bow."
Confidence surges the banks
of his voice: "I hunt for the chase, not the kill."
Doe turns tender towards herself:
"What shall I do with my standing dread?"
Hunter licks the feathers on his
broken arrow (their gleaming pierces her):
"The wind has changed directions."
Doe steps into the meadow.
Hunter is stirred by the girlish way she is
lifting her knees & her saturated
odor. He lets her

come, grateful because the lover gives way
to beloved. Afterwards
when she makes a joke & his laughter flutters
drunk in the sun, they understand
the chase will resume—her bum knee, his one
broken arrow—in spirals so wide,
only the gods can see them.

(iii)
A pervert phones (he knows my name)
just as you & I are talking about

divorce. Of course it won't
work—one breathes in as the other

breathes out. We take our bowls of green tea
into the garden & sit on riverbed

rock. Fossil aquifers seethe
underfoot; poppies guzzle their mandarin

flames; it has not rained for ages.

(iv)
They've grown attached, through sleeping
entwined, at the outer
thigh. He wants to cut loose. She
hands him a blade, gleaming like teeth, he slices

a surgical line—whose blood stains
the blue of their thighs? Who
gags? Who is enraged? Who makes a run for the
outer edge of the world?

At length they agree to forget
each other, heading west & east.
His mind clicks like a digital clock; she
sings outside of the shower.

So circling the globe in counter directions
they're shocked by the sight of a stranger's
thigh—scarred from the hip—
on a train in the heat out of Hong Kong.

(v)
Black satin symphony slides off key.
Strangling in data the species
seems winded, collectively
blind, the poor getting poorer, your nation is selling
arms to the world & your children are planning
their funerals. Cells in the body have all
changed their tune: this
deafening din of revision.

(vi)
"Don't hoard your stuff—"
bag lady sez in the bus
depot. "You're loaded up & your job, lover—
your job is only to empty."

(vii)

"She goes through men like paper plates,"
a castaway crabbed. Every day
a picnic. She daisy chained (she recalls)
her lovers: traded a muse for his madcap
cousin; laughed at a benedict sponging her blood
from his marital weave; teased
the one who loved her like
an emergency; trapped one in a pumpkin
shell; swiveling on barstools, reeled a dreamer (big fish)
over thousands of miles—tore off his lips,
& so on.

After the spree, she swooned in embrace for seven
years, pretending to be an angel.
Actual sprites (memory's girls) rip off her veils
& slap her around, rejoicing
awhile.

(viii)

Gary Snyder hikes with me in a dream
valley. "Cricket/alluvial/strata"—I'm stupid at first
beside him (truth in the names of trees, tools, the deep
well of language)—but chartreuse grasses
spike my feet with mountain
secrets.

I want to kiss him. He
kisses me, sweet like sap in a cypress.
"Is it malarkey, monogamy?"

His grin is lavish headwaters stuff.
"Don't know for you—but always I'm grateful for
sightings of large animals!"

(ix)
There is this pit bull—
he growls, craving meat, he brings me
morsels red in his teeth, he
dogs, shadows me, even
up to the moonlight meadow, the place
we would meet—he scorches me with gloom.
I start from sleep in straightjacket
sheets, yelping his S-shaped
name: Saturn, Senator, Sourpuss—
spinning the volume low at crescendo, he blocks
the thresholds to rooms.

Too late for murder, I pull on my work boots &
clomp around, scaring the cat &
scheming:
          • feed the beast to his liking
              • howl with him, shattering iced stars
                   • vow relentless affection

—which may come to pass: Look
how tenderness softens the stance, the snapping
insatiable snout!

(x)

"Am I," you ask on the long-distance phone, "like an addiction &
you're in a rage because I've been taken away?" This recalls
a woman I know who bought her grandson a pocketknife & fiddling
with it drove the shaft through the plump of her thumb—bloody
point poking out as she turned her trailer upside down in search of
a smoke . . . finally sucking a butt to the nub before dialing 911.

(xi)

The iron law / golden rule / silken
thread of a labyrinth is the psychic
life—cast into darkness &
blinded by sight!

Our solitude is secure.
I know myself yet only crudely, like
the back of my hand.

(xii)

Stopping home on a motorcycle sporting a leather vest
his thoughts are strung with saffron scarves, Latin
guitars, etcetera.

A goldfish skims the crown of the pond, belly up.
She scoops it out, takes it around the side of the house
& drops it among the iris.

Magic carp fishtails away in luminous pool.
Behind her, he's gunning his engine. "Go," she says, "it's OK."
The bars of their prison unzip! like a black dress.

(xiii)
Only
after
we've talked ourselves
mute, snow whirling in blue
parachutes, raven passing squawks a beatitude
through our winter windows.

(xiv)
Each rough rung of the ladder is carved with a monkey's
mug. Primates snatch at my tits & crotch.
Touching down, I drag myself to the gathering.
Men are blissfully lounging against graffitied
walls—the goddess has served them
lotus blossoms & blood cupped in a skull.
I long to go down on my hands & knees, chisel
an airtight tunnel—but this is not what we need.
"Phallus means shining & bright," I hear myself coaxing
(at last she is rocking the ropes of my tongue) "&
you are my darling consorts!"

(xv)

Here it is not the hard breath, bodies as torches
singeing each other, but great sea of being
bleeding through us.

Terra cotta patina dims; the temper drifts
down in the vase & cracks are breaking out along
the meridians. *Love the pitcher less*

& the water more! the Persian poet sings.
We watch from a clearing, our tree bodies smolder,
crushed to fragrance with light.

The Marriage Cloak

(i)
He places a shawl over her shoulders: pink net of
silk and freshwater pearls.

(ii)
Her smile (or maybe it's his) is contagious—
jubilee of O's in the body, act-up chorus of angels.

(iii)
Removing the shawl after thirteen years, cobweb alone
sticks to her skin, its knobs of pearly bone.

(iv)
The smile she casts him is shadowed and chill—
flat stone skipping a lake in a grave hurry to sink.

here's a morning

here's a morning to embrace
(it beats the hell out of last
night, anyway)

& I don't mean

leaky hose
hip-hop crows
cricket up to her thieving knees in black
widow web—I refer to

your absence
your cocksure departure
the square teeth of your smile: "Freedom's
illusion, but marriage for me
is a prison—"

ha ha! ho ho!
tempests & teapots skirt your person like river
rounding rock

the Goddess is livid, Tin Man—
she boots you out of the Temple of Love
on your clever
clattering
ass

& flings me
on the breast of morning
throbbing with insect
& obligation—

sufficient
abundant
sufficient

Penelope Thrashes Herself with Questions

Face to face across a table, mariachi
piped in, tin sconces lining the walls, I ask
so you tell me: her name, her age,
her family and disposition.

Perhaps you forget you are talking to me,
who has loved you. Extravagant language
spills from your mouth: *angel, ease,
transformation.*

At last you pause to ask if I am happy?
"No," I say, "I'm leveled by grief and relief."
I think you remember me for an instant—
before the heavy curtain drops between us.

Penelope Signs

Swathed in a suit, tiger gold, tailored in Havana
he's tanned, maybe 40, leaping boulders
around the lagoon,
approaching.

> *Oh, don't think of sea in lapis July—*
> > *Ionian Neptune sprawled on the deck, your*
> > > *lace bikini draping his jewels—it was*
> > *all the sun-baked water-logged love*
> *you could take!*

They meet at the point where sandy cove is extinguished.
"I've come to ask you for something—."
Her feet are swelling like loaves of bread, ankles of
farm wives in Iowa.

"I'll sign," she says.
Suit lining flashes; he pulls out a packet.

> *Shocking, this thing you ignored*
> > *before: somehow the lover becomes*
> > > *the son,*
> > *stealing*
> *away.*

You and I, Blind as Flames

The push and pull of domestic days
smothers the flame of two—
you and I in the dimming light
could not tell who was who.

I wanted to be your blazing hearth
and you my phoenix lover—
for you there was never lover enough
in any wife or mother.

Alone at the Kitchen Table Addressed by Committee

Sitting alone at the kitchen table
books and papers shoved
aside, you see yourself eating like

someone depressed—slurred
plate, fork hoisted to lips and back
in a careless

ellipsis—pasta muffling the inner body
like staunching a wound
or gagging a bleating sheep.

·

Are you mad at the grain?
These rains, "too little too late"?
Is every thrilling beauty lost to you, then?

Your mongrel body snores on its bones.
Soon you'll be sucking the cold
lips of the dead.

Of course you are grieving! The living
are guilty; the liveliest claw their way to the top
of piled bodies. You only wanted

something sweet to eat.
Yet still we must ask, you must answer.
What is your sacrifice feeding?

Light Splintered from Darkness

Sometimes you wake in an eyelash
moon, weeping.

Nothing has changed.
Your madcap dreams were essentially plain—

yet it is as if savage winds
tear at an unlit wash of subterranean flowers.

You aren't in control, a voice consoles,
you never were.

Star Material

The miner's lungs are satin caskets lined with molybdenum.
Late he emerges, evening's low lavender light
his lone staple of beauty.

Your lungs, like his, have darkened with elements
forged in the workshops of stars. Metallic flecks weighting
the blood, you lean into exhalation.

Suns collapse; seeds explode their containers.
Where to throw your puny weight, these carbon rings of belonging?
Answer the universe, cupping her stars and expanding.

Cowboy Lying Down Cure

Cattle bawling March to November
                vacant and green as the range
                      a cowboy sits his saddle.

Harmonica riffs splintered by dust
                evening settles its precious metals
                around him.

When autumn sleet bites at his bones
                an outlaw chill
                    (blue like the moon)
                    beats down the doors of his chest.

What can he do but hobble his horse
                and throw himself down
                    under awning of oak, dropping away
                        from massing storms
                     the drifting motions of cattle?

                   He tumbles
                through skies of burning
     spurs   a mother's hands   watering holes
                where he and his bovines
                   are sated.

Dissolved in the folds of the earth's
        skirts   a cowboy
        dies or revives.

Dubious Outcomes

Sallow light labors among the apple
boughs.

Out your window, the pumpkin
sleeves of a child's sweater

sifts piled leaves.
What do you know for certain?

Later, the sky may reduce to blue
& you in your sickbed,

drowning.

Hymn to Pneumonia

September stains the windowpanes
diagonally, southwest to northeast

as blood suffuses the glass
stem of a needle.

I watch from the seepy raft of my bed
the lungs labor, seaweed

streaming vaguely away from the light.
My secret is, I am happy.

Nothing needs me but this.
Rain lashes the windowpanes

dispatching drought—O longed for,
protective embrace!

Penelope at the Seashore

for D.R.

The man I loved and bestowed on the sea
strides from the water.

Bronzed and blinkered, bristling sun
he plows a lane across the sand towards

something that wants him.
Standing aside on barnacled rock, I don't even

turn, knowing her flesh beats
with wild birds.

Untold bitterness pools in my mouth: this I spit
in a hard arc to the sea.

Penelope in Winter

not his going but
looming—

starving me down
to winter's

tomb:

rosehip
tuber

cloud
underground.

Penelope Breaking

Treading a threshold's worn tongue
my feet brush the bronze toes of a warrior.

Scalding rivers stream from his flesh: "Speak
if you want me!"

Should I retreat or mock a response, I know
I'll be swallowed by sorrow.

A Sailor Speaks to Penelope

Mountain grasses black with rain, a lad leads me steeply down
to the bucking ship in the harbor.

A mariner, backtracking, falls into step beside me.
He shouts through the tempest, lips to my ear, his drenched gaze
vaulted over the water. "Whatever happens, stay with the ship!
Don't put your faith in a life boat. The mother ship
may even go down—but in the end,
she'll protect you."

Praying for stillness beneath upheaval, I lean to the sailor.
If words can help, these will.

Untitled

The words I long to hear tonight are
Come to bed.

Who receives me anymore by my secret name?

I sleep with a pillow between my thighs
and a Brahms lullabye.

Penelope on the Pier

Grunion-silvered high tide
tarred pilings, carousel gyre, my
dark desire to dive
vs.
reigns between the shoulder blades
tugging back, the shrill
voices of children

Drowning Song

You drop, you suppose, of your own
weight—cannonball lungs
heart hammered
inward, crustaceans
crackling a last
abstraction: *Nothing is personal!*
Sea monsters hatch
in the inked threads of your hair.

Wine Song

I waltz in your arms back through the 19th century, corsets
& burgundy velvet gowns dropped to the floor in a pile
of cognac & smoke. Another time in another place
they are banning displays of Byronic rage, duels at dawn,
the hot pursuit of a barnacled beast on top of an ocean
10,000 times the depth of untested desire. The others
may wish me safe in a house—sofas like animals, grapes &
cheese on porcelain plates & children with shining cheeks—
but I only crave the rasp of your tongue, grasslands
bruised by our spinning feet & clocks of wheat
churning relentlessly backwards

Morning comes (miserable thief) / lipstick
message smeared on the
mirror / silver
snatched /
doors ajar / paramour
wandering the streets in pajamas
& no shoes

After the Fall

Falling into a sewer under the street
you cling to plastic conduit, waiting
to be rescued. A girl who plummeted
close behind croons a lullabye.
Her lover, pursuing, wraps her in his
leather-clad length like a snake.
Left and right along the tunnel, nothing
shines, but a stifled brown luminescence
exudes from above. Thatched together
the lovers make no move to escape.
Once you were trussed like that, too
(a thought sludges through you).
Now you might choose a direction.

I wake in the early morning thinking of you

fir branches ratcheted low with snow
horses stand stock still
listening to moonlight—

sleigh blankets weight my lap
thrown back where you
sat—

wolves howling half circles
just at bay

Tooth & Nail

Trapped in night's metallic barrel I scrape together
a new definition
of you:

> *operator . . .*
>   *hungry ghost . . .*
> *eternal youth . . .*

Captions collapse in morning's cast—yet underground
I struggle with fiends to gain
a sliver of light.

In January the Jilted Painter Sees

Stormy blacks, pelagic
Greens, jagged spits of pale light
Cracking canvas
Edges
And
Dotting the foreground, two
Small figures: his fading, hers
Growing bolder.

Taking Refuge

(i)
Christ in the Desert Monastery, red cliffs by hidden rivers,
seventh day brushing teeth at a row of sinks, a stranger breaks
the silence: "I am on leave from Sisters of Mercy, two months
now. I took my vows as a young ecstatic but over the years my
devotion was poisoned by lust. Even here, in this God-struck
place, amidst the kindness of brothers, I haven't slept a night."

Tiny flames cupped in your hands, you follow her up the piney path
to morning vespers.

(ii)
Driving south for 200 miles . . . Albuquerque . . . Belen . . .
Socorro . . . your passenger's arm gathers sun at the window.

(iii)
The San Mateos shoulder snow. You park on the gravel loop
of the refuge, pile on jackets and mount the platform
as cannonball sun comes roaring with snow geese—tens of
thousands pulled from the sky, honking and calling they settle
to fields of flooded grain like bridal veils exhaling over a bed.

(iv)
Later in a rented room, in a town named for succor, the lover's
embrace bestows absolution—which rescues you, for awhile.

Dear Goddess

Dear Goddess, I have forgotten
your earthen tongue
cloud womb
the way to draw close
and drop down.

Dead gods bicker in beds
of stone.
My torn arrow
slackens in circles flung
far from the target.

Envelope me, Mother, heave me
hard to your
mountainous breasts,
the deep
seas of your heart.

The Widow Waking

The widow in her shoreless bed knows she is dreaming.
Drifting to darkness in untethered skiffs, sailors bail; tortoise
devoured, they ration ruined bread.

Her captain floats alone in a boat with an ebony girl.
His hands, shadowed by diva sea, are boney chalices
cupping blood: "Drink, my beauty!"

Autumn rows towards equinox across the attic floor.
Lines of thought the widow would hold, scull into shadow.
Saltwater gulfs the blue bones of her ankles.

In Praise of Margaritas

for A.L.

(i)
Summer solstice, mid-life, two women in patio chairs,
bare legs & plain toes angled towards the perfect breast of
Sun Mountain—undulant sweep of cedar & pine
basking in twilight.

(ii)
One announces her former husband is parked on a mountain
picnicking with the kids. There will be blue jays (crudest
of vandals), talk about soccer, sexy cars, the relative virtues of
mustard & relish, but not a word of her.

(iii)
The other ex will have knocked off work in the next town—
he'll visit the gym, order a hero sandwich to-go & a video.
Probably then he thinks of their son, coming down
for the weekend; without her, they'll have some fun.

(iv)
The women are downing margaritas on the rocks,
theme of the evening. Sun Mountain feathers herself in darkness.
The tired houses of their mouths fall into ruin,
struggle to reconfigure.

(v)

Rubenesque pitcher drained of tequila & plush air fractured
by laughter, one says her ex is chasing a train, packed with
fertile women: *"Wait!"* he is waving behind the caboose—
"Wait, I'm coming, you need me!"

Hot Potato

Now there's a question I'm burning to put
to Wife #1: "What did you love
about him?"

She'll only remember fragments: surge of limbs
on a Portuguese beach, treetops
at dawn, his animal ease
with children.

Just as quickly, she'll toss the question back
in my lap: "And what did *you*
love about him?"

Spooked of their shadows my routed memories
crowd into hers: bodies of water,
sons like saplings,
his beauty.

Who Can Tell?

I'm staring at the stranger's feet in turquoise satin slippers
wondering: What would be the size of his member
relative to those several inches?

The dwarf meanwhile is climbing over me, deftly sliding under
the covers, he stretches his length from the nape of my neck
to my flexed knees—one petit muscled arm

presses my breathless waist.
Well, who can tell? *Whatever* arises between lovers
comes as a great surprise.

hour of the wolf

3:40 a.m.
the vessel wakes me, burning
calories: green curry
fat strips of filet mignon
two glasses of good Merlot

under hip & shoulder
mattress oval
hot as a nest in matted snow
where wolf bitch
has been sleeping

the obvious outcome of
excess: last night, four friends
talking & tasting
drinking & laughing, three hours
linked at the table

almost as if there were no
apparitions—dispatched husbands
listing among us
casting their tacky gossamer nets
to catch the breath

The Cruelest Month

All morning
      savage winds
            wring the necks
                  of daffodils, knell
      the bell in the wall.

O tulips,
      lay low,
            bind your colors, pray
                  for respite—a stay
      of execution!

Spring Tide

You come for dinner bearing fruit from Farmers Market
dressed in shorts, your blue tank top, a new
tattoo. Under chipped enamel lid, a stew
simmers: onions, carrots, finger potatoes, meat
stewed in its juices. I lead you out to see my garden
freshly hoed into rows. April air

teases the body—*trust me!* Our teenager
reads from the Sunday comics, a joke about
poets and money. I rant awhile against a neighbor; you
talk about salsa lessons. Stew ladled to big-mouthed
bowls, French baguettes, a young beaujolais,
we dine on the patio, wrought-iron table

rocking under our elbows. Our knees
touched for thousands of nights under this table;
sometimes I'd drink and drop into anger.
The telephone rings, you think of the long drive home.
I hand you your mail, walk with you out
to the numbered curb, receive the familial kiss.

After a death the tide goes out and
doesn't return—we must walk from island to island.

Cloudburst in Early May

Afternoon cloudburst dousing drought
you stand on a round of new lawn

drinking rain and chardonnay
lightning gashes the southern sky

behind a neighbor's maple
mechanical church bells clang "Ave Maria"

porch edged in purple penstemon
hummingbird moths hover

one rogue sunbeam glitters green
yesterday you were grieving

up the street octagonal STOP
red as Carmen's lips

bare feet in tender grass
riverbed replenishing

Tara's Poem

Half-way through this laboring night
tumbling from sky into alpine
village, no-one holding
the end of my string, I make a prayer
to undoing: make
confetti of dead
wishes; marry a lunatic under a bower
of burning roses; bow
to the goddess
only: Make every breath a prayer.

What Is Given

The spacious gong of a man's voice
wakes me, speaking

my name—the old-fashioned
simple syllable of it.

Vitality brims the doorway.
I stand on elbow: "What is it?"

All I can see are rounds and rectangles,
furniture limned by starlight.

Pad to the kitchen, pour water, drink
in the dark. Snow-kicked

moonlight fuses the window, silvers
the rim of the glass.

What does it *want*, this voice?
I know, at least, what it *gives*:

Shocking pleasure of hearing my name
clearly spoken; cold tile

underfoot; ribbons of
river and snow.

This moment is given, this poem.

His New Wife

Bursting out of her blueberry skin gleaming with butter and youth
she stands in the kitchen that's hers now, assembling
a casserole. Wide mouth like a bowl of cream

she wraps you in an eau de toilette abrazo.
Your former husband hands you a glass of tea.
"Siéntate! Siéntate!" his bride insists.

She's spooning mayonnaise smooth to the pan's lip.
*"Es arróz, camarones, más arróz, jamón, hamburguesa, queso y
pues—más queso!"*

Spanish rushing over the dam, el marido must translate: "Her
papa's a cook in Havana; she says she's not a very good cook—"
"Pero si mi amor no se le gusta, el puede llevarme al restaurante!"

His smile a bleak appointment.
He hinges a kitchen cabinet door; screwdriver crowned by gold
wedding ring—low in your gut a stab of resentment,

then nothing. He'd worn a band with you, for awhile, until
it was stolen (he'd always believed) by the Mexican maid who'd
wept as she scrubbed, longing for her children in Chihuahua.

Romantic Love

Heaving sheets of sapphire sea, peaks
and troughs like the Himalayas—
no way to know where you are
in such immensity.

Coursing by on a spit of water, someone
becomes a buoy. Sea relaxes,
warms to the blood, abysmal demons
all fall asleep.

"Land!" you exclaim to your darling in arms,
heedlessly drifting towards it.

Hungry Ghost

What do you think you are doing, hanging
around my dreams? Recently

you shot my father (who's already dead)
accidentally, a stray bullet. And last night

how thrilled you were, sexy letters
addressed to you, linked like sausages

spat from my fax machine.
Dream fractured, I beg you:

Why won't you leave me alone?
You are counting piles of counterfeit money.

I'm trying, you answer, *believe me.*
But you are my landmark in No Man's Land—

I only look back to get my bearings,
and you refuse to recede.

After Completion

After completion
ashen offering cupped in your hands
a fugitive gust from out of the blue

and poof!—

Not like dandelion spores
or dispersal of sequins retrievable
one by one, but manifest

disappearance.

You fix your feet with bags of cement
and think like the devil.
How to interpret this transfiguration

without interference from angels?

New Year's Eve, Rome, Italy

What could they possibly say to each other, lovers
descending cobblestone steps, kissing
on sculpted bridges?

A shuttered siesta; then tippling celebrants
clog Roman streets.

There's no nostrum for failed memory, ruined flesh, flash
point wars in the Middle East, your habit of acquiescence
and betrayal.

Roman candles rip the sky and arc into beauty,
towards you.

End of the Line

A woman without a prayer
boards a train leaving a city
tunneling under a river

perched in desperate yellow light
horizon seesaws
landscape shreds to dim pastels

brakes squeal doors slide
under the sagging shoulders of corn
she starts to walk

Sex & the Lake

(i) SENSUAL TRIUMPH

You come upon a lake, river
fed, blue ache at the crusty knees of
a desert—100 miles of Permian sand slipped like
silk from the bolt, easy to reach the edge of it—plunge
deep, press to the mentholate center, micaceous slip, you turn
in a lover's hands.

               Splayed
         in the dunes
           later,
                  your pores guzzle rays of sun
        as regents, powdered in gold dust
receive a stream of suppliants.

(ii) BALM WITHOUT SALVATION

When did the river go underground
at either end of the lake? You honor its
resourcefulness, draining hidden rivulets, sloughing
sediment, mineral, sunbath, in absent love with the sea.
You come to the lake as a beggar, no begging bowl
but the body: holding hands, you wade into water—gasp of
surprise!—parchment flesh unfurls
like a baby's fists.

      Afterwards
    you are sifted
       into a sand
         painting—ochre, rust
   & soothing pinks, the
grounded gestures of snow angels.

What Does It Mean to Say Married?

My Uncle Tom married his Betty when they were 18. He moved her off the family farm for a life in Chicago, then back to the land. At 80, he told us: "Betty's the only woman I've known, the only one I need." Today he wanders the shadowy country of Alzheimers. "What's happening, Betty? Do you know where we're going?" Tenderly, his wife reassures him, "Yes, Tommy, I do," over and over. Other couples, of two minds, tell conflictual stories. Ringing under the argument, though, a syncopation—chain gang striking obdurate ground with blunted picks and shovels. Day by day we must start in again: the back grows muscled, the mind goes to rhythm and blues.

Story of Woman Y

Woman Y is thrown in the lap of Stranger X for no apparent reason. Impulsively, she pledges conjugal love; X confides his plan to kill the insurance agent. Gamely, Y conspires—they'll bury him in the vineyard & disappear with the proceeds. By midnight they're married, the victim is casketed under the nuptial roses . . . but sudden antipathy renders the couple anathema to each other. Worse yet, Central Office deduces the murder & phones in the morning to say they'll be over to make a double arrest. Woman Y withdraws to her ablutions. Wrapped in a towel she peers out the upstairs window. The groom & hungover wedding guests are shouting "Marco Polo!" in the swimming pool. A fleet of squad cars shackles the gravel drive. Woman Y massages her flesh with scented oil. This could be her last respite for many years— 8 to 10, if she slants the facts so that X takes the rap & she is his passive accomplice.

It Falls to Me

It falls to me to put an end to my youngest child's
life—he has been stabbing strangers, dream
authorities say, whenever they make comments
he dislikes. He is grown, a man turned
fat and perverse, but after
I sink the blade to the hilt in the jugular vein
he's four once more, piccolo voiced and pure.
"My blood smells like a jungle," he murmurs.
I pull a blanket under his chin, kiss his cheeks, rake
fields of baby hair with trembling fingers.

Wake in a mummy sleeping bag in the back of a car
parked in a sacred canyon—sky
decked in its gaudiest jewels so even the blind
might see them. I think of my friend
from Korea, rocked to sleep in her boat of a house
for the dreamless years after her son—the one
with the glorious smile—hung himself in his dormitory
at Amherst. Stars pierce my porthole of steam.
And in between, intervals speak to the turned out
pockets of innocence.

Sonnet for Spring in a Time of War

Folding chair, back corner, last seat in the house
I sip from a smuggled bottle of beer
and weep as I please—
when a warden kisses a prisoner's throat . . .
when a girl sprawled on African ground speaks a lyric poem . . .
when a sorrowing man goes off to war to slay his soul . . .

Emerging to spring in the high desert
the moon's a silver spoon
air whispers and opens
Kenyans are singing rounds to the moon, they drink
from a cow's belly
I ditched the peace protest tonight—
stop the car on a rutted lane and break off
an armload of lilacs

Blossoms swarm beside the bed in swan-necked pitcher:
every petal connected to every other

daybreak

crows bite the night into day
claiming resources
naming boundaries—Kashmir,
Sudan, Croatia, Tibet—
mountain corsets shaken loose
cross-hatch of fallen bodies,
consciousness splits like a river

America, Married Woman

America, married woman, sleeps shuttered,
pays taxes, acquaints herself with the daily news
but fails to notice her solar system expands
beyond cognition—one ringed planet
jumping orbit.

She sleeps in the arms of the status quo, dreaming
of ladders and shapes in the yard—crocodilians
older than Moses, eyelids
cocked over mineral orbs, those
oiled, guillotine jaws.

Ordinary News

Rumble of dawn delivery runs: produce; newspapers; sunup
parade of pickup trucks, hardhats & sacks of three-penny nails
riding the bench seats.

Already my house is busy with flies, sentient beings
I can't kill (though Buddha knows I want to). Somebody's droning
mother or other pursues me from room to room.

Mean in speech & manner last night, I suffer remorse.
"Try to be kinder to one another," Aldous Huxley chided in his dying.

Grandfather hackberry shades the drive, nippled with gall maker
due to drought. Resident ravens couldn't care less,
claiming the crown branches.

Middle age arrived like a season: predictable, unsuspected.
Stunned as a summer adolescent, I drift towards vigia.
What is the shape of that which can neither be

known nor avoided? I hustle a pair of mating flies towards the open
door; newspaper fan throttles the daily news.

10,000 Joys 10,000 Sorrows
(Instructions to Myself)

1.

Resist falling back asleep, the loveliness
of butter knives over the body.

2.

Fix on the wren with the eight-note song,
the child blowing her nose and singing.

3.

Boatloads of Haitians dumped in the sea—
you venture another list.

4.

10,000 joys 10,000 sorrows, everything
begs your attention.

5.

Choose what quickens, move in close,
be transfigured.

eggs

2 eggs slip your fingers
splash linoleum
last 2 the chickens could give

no frittata no cake
no supper soufflé
the evening will be subdued

but low in the solar plexus
a golden egg

Jack's Mother Leaving

My son, his fiancée and I, are snuggled together
in a dream—singing hills, plants that can

speak, a freeway system with woven exits
like Persian puzzle rings.

The lock is too tight; I break it by waking.
There's Jack out the south window

appraising his beanstalk, looping to cirrus cloud.
I slip on a shift, old shoes, one pin for my hair.

Colors of sunrise doused by plains, screen door
claps at my back.

Farewell, my Jack—I am taking the smallest seed.

Drought

for Catherine

(i)
Hard snow weighting the earth, they ordered
a backhoe to dig a place in the orchard
for Bill—his daugher, her mother, and Catherine
his former lover, gripping blanket corners
lowered him down, bathing his corpse
in tears and shoveled dirt.

(ii)
The voluptuous earth was impossible not to adore.
Early on, Bill surrendered—scaling mountains,
crisscrossing badlands, sleuthing for mushrooms,
a rare bird, plant retracted from bovine jaw, the steel
tooth of tractor. Sometimes he'd come to the lip of a stream
and drop to his knees, laughing: *I'm here, my beloved!*

(iii)
Beleaguered by cancer, at last he conceded:
I give you my body.

(iv)
Lankily underpinning the orchard, he tracks Catherine
late in July, dipping and bobbing, her long hair
tipped with paint, kaleidoscope
staining an adamant
sky—*the rains*, Bill assures her,
will come.

Some Days

"Some days are better than others . . ."
my father answered the visiting nurse, curving
above him, her snowcapped breasts—Oh, inhalation
of flowery flesh!—his last afternoon on earth.

My father occurs in the rushing darkness of stars.
On failed days, I recall his perfect words.
He trusted in science, earth as you find her, rhythms of
unbroken work.

Some days are better than others.
A crimson hibiscus, gold flecked, bloomed out of season
outside the door of my father's house
the fine night of his dying.

because our breasts are landscapes of endless joy

because our breasts are saltwater swells
furred animals
dunes strewn with sand dollars
ruffled by wind crescendos

because for a spell they are pleasure lures
sunned fruits turned in the hands
fountains for infants, figments
for aged men

because they are tugged by gravity's lips
savaged by illness—chiseling
scalpels, X's
scarred on the torso

out of the blue in a checkout line
an infant cries and our breasts
become rivers—phantom flesh, roughly used, yet
tenderly, earth remembers

breath after breath

breath after breath
        after breath I have loved
                break of morning, sky hoisting
                        starry skirts &
                          soiled petticoats, Earth
              reclined on blue
        divan, smelling faintly of
sex & fennel & milk

Dog and Monkey

When Dog lets Monkey into her lair they trade stories
and tidbits of information. Next visit they draw closer, drink
whiskey, giddy laughter and so on. Monkey charms with
chatter and gymnastics. Dog, stretched in a yoga pose,
studies her suitor's scent.

Before you can say *Jack Robinson!* Monkey arrives
with a couple of bags and some tools. His family photos
go up on the walls; he fixes a number of broken fixtures
and dazzles his darling by feeding her oysters with
nimble, opposable thumbs.

Primate and canine fall to their folly with careless abandon.
But after a time, character trumps desire. Dog, doggedly
propped on her haunches, watches the quiet door; Monkey
dreams he is flying through trees, hitched
to a tropical breeze.

Any Tear in the Social Fabric

Any tear in the social fabric leaves
a dangling trail.
The village ne'er-do-well, for example,
steals a pig and hides her in his potato cellar
hoping that such audacious action
will go unnoticed.
Instead—lo! a jagged arrow
appears in the air
pointing down at the culprit's head—
the villagers come at a dead run
screaming obscenities, hurling
dirt and manure.
The thief insists he only meant
to borrow the pig.
Here the sow's rightful owner, a ruddy widow
with ice-pick eyes, incites
violence: "Stone the thief!"
The pig squeals at her voice.
The motley mob of brothers & cousins
are riled, but reluctant.
What happens next is anyone's guess . . .
but afterwards, like film in reverse,
things revert to normal.

When You Meet Your Former Husband on a Road

(after a story told by Andrew Harvey)

An Indian girl of six or seven, walking on a road near her village,
sees a man she recognizes. Shantih approaches him boldly:
"I was your wife in my former life. Our house
was down beside the fields, a kilometer from the well.
The flavors you loved were cardamom and mint.
Our money is hidden behind the altar—you'll find it there."

Hastening home, the stranger sits alone in his garden,
engulfed by oceans.
His new wife brings him tea in a mustard bowl.
He doesn't look for the money at once, knowing it's there.
The storm at last recedes into essence: two drops, like purest rain,
one containing the other.

After meeting the man on a road, Shantih remembers another
world and the Lord Krishna. *"Now, daughter, return to your people.
Tell them about the afterlife, so they can have faith."*
As for the stranger, familiar to her as father or brothers,
recognition doesn't touch her knowledge of pleasure—baking pita,
wading the river, braiding her mother's hair.

Castanets in carob leaves clatter Krishna's praises. *"Yes, Shantih!
When you meet your former husband on a road, respectfully
tell him what you know, wish him well,
then run home to your mother!"*

Victor Arthur

A-train swallowed by subway tunnel spits you out on the platform. Younger cousin of Orpheus leads you up from under the earth, never a backward glance. Straggling behind, blocks unravel through lower Manhattan; five flights up a fire escape, you haul your exhaustion through his open window.

The rooms of your host are wired for science and sound. One is spread with a cape of neon blue. Language somersaults off his tongue, you can't understand—until he commands (*sotto voce*), "Come to bed." You like his brown Samoan feet, the broad plains of his thighs, but every action counts now and you're at a loss. "I don't even know your name!" His face a relief of irony and intent: "My name is Victor Arthur."

A day or two passes and Victor Arthur has left the apartment. Surely, you bore him. As others arrive, you scramble down the fire escape and enter a red-lit cafe. No one about, chairs leaning into the tables, you choose a booth with a basket of yesterday's bread.

Victor Arthur slides in beside you, his thighs like locomotives. "You thought you could give me the slip?" Louie and Ella goof from the juke: "You say potatoes and I say potatoes!"—you jump up to dance among the drunken chairs. Cousin of Orpheus catches you up, for several measures you move together and then you are down on blue linoleum, diamonds and flesh, the rolling crush of bone. Words break from the jailhouse of your throat: "My big Victor Arthur, you won't need to show me home!"

What You See (Is Always Less Than What You Get)

Driving west into plummeting
sun, you glimpse
a face behind the wheel

of a green
truck—contemplative, rugged,
5 or 6 decades—and

something at your center
opens, an indigo
paper fan.

Turning north you notice how
the pleasure shape
remains.

Not your father, not
your brother, not a former lover but
a face belonging to you.

Now and then
a piece fits the puzzle, degrees are
exact, plumb bob

drops through fathomless seas,
you are rocked
in your mother's arms.

Lilacs Again

for T.I.

Spring winds dragged by the sun beyond the low horizon
your land exhales like a woman squatting alone in a field
resting between contractions.

A man in blue hospital scrubs waits for an empty bus.

You turn on a lane where years ago you pirated
armloads of lilacs. The branches are damp under the bark
where you tear them.

Colophon

Set in VAN DIJCK, a typeface created by the Monotype
Corporation in 1935 under the direction of Stanley Morison.
This revival by Jan van Krimpen (1892-1958) is based on
the types of Christoffel van Dijck (1606-1669). Van Dijck was
considered a superb craftsman and a leading punch-cutter of
Amsterdam. His designs were used successfully by the renowned
Elzevir publishing firm in Leyden for many of their Greek &
Roman texts. This version attempts to capture van Dijck's
sense of Oldstyle dignity and robust sturdiness —"to be read
easily and to wear well"—while integrating van Krimpen's
subtle curvilinear touches and resonant color. *The italic was
modeled after an edition of Ovid printed in 1671.* Van Krimpen's
type designs have been criticized, though, for being more
from "an inner vision, not from a broad view of practical
realities and requirements," but sometimes
beauty is function.

Long time New Mexico resident, Anne Valley-Fox worked as a Poet-in-the-Schools with New Mexico Arts during the 1970s and 1980s. Since 1986, she has been a writer-researcher for Project Crossroads, a creative educational resource group based in Santa Fe. She is co-author with Sam Keen of the nonfiction work *Your Mythic Journey: Finding Meaning in Your Life through Writing and Storytelling* (Jeremy P. Tarcher/Putnam, 1989; Bantam audiotape, read by the authors, 1992). Her poems are collected in *Sending the Body Out* (Zephyr Press, 1986) and a special issue of *Fish Drum Magazine* (1999); and appear in the anthologies *New Mexico Poetry Renaissance* (1994); *The Best of Mothering: 1976-1996* and *In Company: New Mexico Poets after 1960* (UNM Press, 2004). She lives in Santa Fe, New Mexico.

Photograph by Nan Adams